My Funeral Gondola

My Funeral Gondola

Fiona Sze-Lorrain

MĀNOA BOOKS • EL LEÓN LITERARY ARTS
HONOLULU • BERKELEY

My Funeral Gondola is copublished by

Mānoa Books, an imprint of The Mānoa Foundation (themanoafoundation.org)
Frank Stewart, Publisher
Interior design and composition by Peak Services
(peakservices.squarespace.com)

El León Literary Arts
(elleonliteraryarts.org)
Thomas Farber, Publisher
Kit Duane, Managing Editor

Distributed by Small Press Distribution, Inc.
1341 Seventh Street
Berkeley, CA 94710
800-869-7553
www.spdbooks.org

Available on Amazon.com

ISBN 978-0-98339198-2
Library of Congress Control Number 2012953362
Printed in the United States of America

Cover image: *Clouds* (1920–26) by Claude Monet. Musée de l'Orangerie, Paris, France. Printed by permission of Art Resource, Inc.

Contents

III Not Thinking About the Past

In this yard I was happier than you'll ever know.
Neighbors, I wish you all long lives.

Nazim Hikmet

Sixteen Lines, Autumn 2010

In past autumns, I saw the world differently.

Swans looked graceful
because their bodies were white.

Crows were soothsayers — black
wings, black cries.

In those autumns, death was a small affair.
One leaf fell.
Another.

This autumn, death gets even smaller.

Leaves tilted by wind, into ashes of the earth.
Swans grow fatter,
dropping two or three feathers
into water.
Crows, mouthing air in bare elder trees.

Look: a long sundown.

No more black and white.

I | *The Title Took Its Life*

Notes from My Funeral

Faces.
Anonymous guests
invited where a buffet awaits
with dragon fruit, salmon maki,
baked apricots, olives, ginger
duck… My favorite food is served
after African odes. Tibetan
chants end a virtual
sky burial. With respect
to my Irish governess, a priest
will be there. Alas,
he still can't pronounce
my name in full.
Thirty years my senior, my husband finds
his seat. On a bench at the back,
a permanently sad smile
and thirty years of thoughts.
For the first time, without pedal
and trills, my pianist brother
mixes up Liszt with Dylan.
My coffin is round.
Perfect *fengshui.*
I lie like Leonardo's Vitruvian Man.
The sound of wild gods drumming in my heart.
I settle where the wind
blows me. From one state of gratitude
to another province.
Eyes unshut. I wait
for the flowering of my last
wish, *The honor of your presence*
is requested at your own funeral
reception. RSVP.

My Death

Someone weeps. Laughs. Or screams.
Grief cannot be quarantined — it must
be a battle.

Already retired, my death
now prepares
its act without weapons.

Radical and revolutionary.

Like a fly
diving into a bowl of black
rain. Experience

this bleeding cloak, a one-time

appearance.

Karma

This is the ninth moon.

Fog rises in knots, with necessary pain.

A beggar believes in fortune,
Give me, give me.

He follows a hand, a plume of smoke,
a rope bridge

that shakes on its own.

In this life, suffering is nothing.
I'll grant you a wish,

hungry ghosts —

statues that knock at my stone gate.

My Melancholy

moves from window to window

between calendars

on Mid-Autumn Festival, it vanishes

like moons and peaches under startled lanterns

promising us official secrets

My Nudity

delivers what is important
and unimportant
about my body, between action
and repose, at room
temperature.
I never pose like Athena.
Nor like the statue of Madame Lucrezia.
Smile in progress, but
no emotion.
Nothing *extraordinaire,*
just a mild detail,
a birthmark, a loud hip
bone. If I take a toe
in my mouth, elegance
isn't streamlined.
My skin takes thoughts
away from light.
Before this mirror, I am my painter,
realizing that bareness
opens
and never shuts.
What is pride? The image inside us.
Thank you, mole,
for behaving like an ink
drop, spreading
invisibly
from a visible site,
a hole
that trembles and tickles
from inside.

Now, Meditate

Yes, the nostrils of silence.
A sea of visitors chained together.
More or less tempting
melancholia.
I no longer know my kind.
Light added to light, mountains feel near.
What is darkly denied us?
Let it go,
this chestful of sky.
My stomach turns from stone
to birds.
Pain washes one or two moons down my back.
I listen.
Bones are now moving alike.

Diva

She sings about secrets taken to the grave,
her voice scattering an octave to eight winds.
She claims she opens her windows with no ulterior motive,
improvising the same chanson according to weather.
When the phone rings, she answers *Allegro ma non troppo*.
She listens to her silent *fin-de-siècle* radio,
saves an aria for the postman returning undelivered mail.
From heroine to villainess, her arms flutter in two
different colored, over-the-elbow satin gloves.
She pours cough syrup into her Chanel handbag.
Toying with the position of a fake mole on her face,
she eats her scores when she can't recall
her past triumphs at *Theater am Kärntnerto,
Wiener Staatsope, Opéra de Paris*...
With an assassin's smile, she waters her plants
while scratching her armpits.
Purple lipstick means she bit her lip
by accident, chewing on a pear
carved out of porcelain.
From the balcony, she drains macaroni.
Do not insult her *folle*, she'll weep and call an ambulance.
Empty demijohn clasped in her bosom, she hiccups
and sleepwalks down the corridor.
Yesterday she was Catherine the Great
in undersized sheath dress and green push-up bra.
Today she metamorphosizes into Athena
draped in second-hand, ready for an audience.
Come, let's take a picture for an exclusive!
Not so close-up please, slightly farther...
Who are you?
Beatrice. Magda. Gretchen or Julia.
Röslein, Röslein, Röslein rot—

When the Title Took Its Life

My saddest lines
wish to know how they left
this pen

and why I imprison them
in corridors
along margins. Abbreviated

but exhausted from labor.

Tonight, they wreak revenge
on my mortal hand—

Erase me.

Write, "I don't know
why I am sad.
Night is long. Like an empty house
with annexes of silence."

Or bar with a slash
words like "bleeding,"
"persecution," "exile," and "loneliness."

Like a blind judge, these lines
doubt my sincerity.
Here is not life.

The sickle moon looks down.

What does it know? The storm
I heard when I meant
to be writing.

Listening to Tchaikovsky, Rain Suddenly Pours

Many fingers caught in invisible
webs, a museum of spiders
struggle to waltz. Insecure chords
cloak silence in pleas, a
winter that couldn't end
and permanent grief.
Napoleon tore himself apart in 1812.
Stalled between trumpet calls
and cannon shots,
notes were transformed
into corpses,
half-devoured dogs,
the weight of hunger and something
lost. I am supposed to transcribe
the coda of this wrong. A tragedy
Tchaikovsky managed
to score. This assignment
became a small cause
for an afternoon
ruined in Hamburg. I stared
out a balcony of my white
guesthouse. The rain came
harder and in person,
from different directions
and voiceless. The rain
came harder, from the middle
of somewhere, of
nowhere, like an orchestra
of spiders, frozen
and eyeless
at my empty funeral.

My Funeral Gondola

has nothing to do

with Liszt
with Wagner
with Tranströmer

it positions itself
midway in a strait — so that shadows
in a trance

by the woods
by the sun

travel over it, like an arraignment of locusts

draped in their pleas
leaving behind the coffin
an architecture

smuggled by my sons

an object of meditation
a fact
when light blares

II | *Odd Spirits*

Orion

Before death the seer showed me how
you eluded mystery

by the harbor where lights
were ill at ease

through the emptiness worn
to transparency

leaving behind a nest

of children vying for truth
the peace they startle

with their existence

Javanese Wayang

First, smoke. The elders grope
into the theater. Like hidden

bronze mirrors, midnight lanterns
glow. I don't ask

when the play begins. Ocher moths
over the whiteness

of the screen where trees clutch
the hungry rain, running

after wrong spirits. Someone is making
room for the wind. Inexplicable,

long fingers of light drag up a torn
hero. Self by self, he steals

away from his body. *Gamelan* enters:
the neighborly dark

roams. Watch the shadows, not
the puppets.

Still in the Night Fields of Hokkaido

Inattentive rain. Inattentive star.

Water and light in this violent faint
life. The fields, say

the ancients, an unwinged sea
of lamps. In the space,
concentric silence expanding

outwards. Into the stillness,

and on into distance. Crickets question

twice. They register an air
between real and improvised time.

Crickets — I can't
finish my line. Nature suddenly

feels so foreign

and I just broke my camera.

Monuments Against Sundown

Clouds abandon the memory of light. Cryptic shapes of yes and
no, they know the flaws of twilight from all centuries. Stillness
grows. The evening inherits a soliloquy of black trees. In this
place, you are nobody. What reason can you give for the
underworld? It is right here because you're drawn to it. A man
doesn't walk with his ghosts. He walks with his shadow, the man
who says no. And he stops, not because he falls. He stops because
the ugly moon is glued into the sky, and in this treason of light,
seagulls land and cry.

François Dead

Without improvisation, we empty the drawers.
Papers slip. He pulls the shades, lifts
the mattress, dismantles
the Victorian bed. I wash the floor
with a rag on all fours.
After arranging those famous first-
editions, we stop and fold
silence into a cigarette.
He lights the lamp, we return to dust.
When his back gives way, he says we must
rest. *What's this?* A musty hardcover
of ancient elegies
loosely translated from the Japanese.
François said he stole it.

Cremating Maestro

Sixteen, I understood the death of Li Po
not by gazing at his immaculate moon
nor by grieving the jade tree in his odes
clouds withheld by provisional verbs,
a shallow silence in commas. Scholars
claimed that he was drunk, extravagantly,
like a general who fell at triumph's end.
Lordly in his strength, the poet usurped
rage and the brevity of rain. Historians
saw a better end — they preserved his boat,
framed reasons for his bipolar sadness —
set loose his hair in a failing light.

Sixteen, I folded a paper boat for you,
imagining it once carried Li Po, imagining
it was his body, floating somewhere
to reach somehow, a weightless departure
in dispraise of judgment. Not the shore,
but this fishing in the air. Like last foxgloves,
everyone bowed, waiting for your soul
to split in white silence. I looked up. Saw
the painful moon. The one that witnessed
the return of few gods. The one you evoked
in a last smoke, "That's where Li Po went home."

"After great pain, a formal feeling comes —"

Emily Dickinson

Outside is barely above zero. Poor visibility, makeshift
mountains. For strange reasons I see Lake Toba. A volcano from
Java out of all this ice. There is a fishing boat, a mirage island. A
thousandfold sun and a clarity frozen. I don't know why these
images return. They are pulling a meridian in fright. I can't
ignore them but it is alright. Will you label them *reckoning* this
time? A word that means something if you still keep faith. In
this poem, you want names and details. Real and precise. It
depends on luck. Or boundaries. When our son died, we kept
the ghosts in mind, baking cakes for guests who sat like cats
through the wake.

Lullaby

A storm acts like a rehearsal from another angle. Visualize ghosts chasing dogs on a rooftop, this was how I trained my brother not to fear thunder. These days he teaches his patients that lightning looks animal. One of them is a mother who talks to the Stove God. She prays for a city and blanched babies. How do you deal with those who carry their tombs through voices and moonlight? And those seeking permission from loneliness? Questions persist as my brother lowers the curtains in a kitchen that prepares meals for vegetarians. His answer is fast and dimensional. Never mind. Bees multiply. Troubles will hide. Even hands fly.

Neither an Elegy Nor a Dream

My grandfather caught a tiger in a stone, and could carve a
stone into a tiger. He was not an angry man. He built bridges
and cupboards. Leaving behind twelve rabbits and a foundation.
The bed he made for me surrendered its shape when my body
suspended a mountain in me. Now and then I asked the door if
he'd return with the clothes he died in. His noble face, too
discreet to weep. The shaman believed I betrayed my
clairvoyance. *Quick, swallow all the coins you've stolen.* The dead
always punish odd spirits. In my sleep, a vulture was arranging
its feathers at my feet. I fidgeted but held my laughter.
Premonition ended like a fruit fallen. In defeat, in plain colors.
My grandfather initiated our pact. No time to fall ill, no time to
heal. I wasn't young, but I was forgiven. I took the same road,
braved the same sun. I rode on shadows and looked for white.
Trying to memorize our last time.

Again from Nowhere, Or This Time from Somewhere

Wind blows away his organs, and a canyon in his body. This is a
Chinese verse I translated last night. One the sacred voices say
never stops half-way. Ask why the wind must come uninvited. Or
how it contemplates a past in stillness. As if this morning it
embodies new details. As if today it performs a second ritual. Not
that my senses hold grievances against it. Wind isn't a tradition
you learn to tame unruly souls. It teaches us to outgrow our
madness. To abandon distance, to fall prey to dirt. Leading us to
deserts where thoughts shouldn't have stayed. In the house of
wind, no table is fixed. Like the spirits, I am not a fatalist. I wake
up thinking of leeks on an omelette. Should I open a jar of ginger
jam. When Natsuko phones, she is hiding with her son. In a
cupboard, wrapped in kimonos and sacks. Their earth is now
unmade and continues to shake. She quotes the wind as two
minutes and says the clock is wrong.

Scarlet

Say orchids. *(You're orchids.)*

Say the forbidden. *(You're the forbidden.)*

An Indian told me orchids keep themselves sober. A lucidity
short of thoughts but free from culture. Five petals in a hierarchy
of answers, darkening by the glare. Look for the drunken ones
when your road is clear. I'm not sure why orchids remind me of
her. The way she served us tea, thin without sugar. What does a
kingdom of orchids weather? The eye of a guest orbiting in
seduction.

Sonata Amorosa

quasi una fantasia

1. Must We Meet

Tired of clouds even a mystery
to the sky,
I seek someone sharp
at high moon. No small talk

as introduction —
you bring the other world in an invisible mode.
So invisible
that I must walk to it in an invisible

coat. Not the words as fact,
but the voice,
same yet different in each
revised letter. Actor and spectator,

in roles interchanged. A romance happens
as a question of hours.
No ink, no paper
as a witness. Even trains…No,

they forget here. Why the discretion,
I can't say.
We begin with Rimbaud,
travel to Venice, describe white tigers,

disavow an afterlife.
Are you a chair or a table.
Always the impression I come close
to your time,

your aura, your remove
in emptiness —
thoughts on the horizon that imitate
rainy sentences,

fragile memorials,
contingent on this happiness
or weather,
There is no loud end in a healing distance.

2. The New Deal

Once my husband falls asleep, I start to smuggle
rhapsodies under our blanket.
Sometimes, the effort proves to be as excruciating
as birth labor. It measures itself
through seconds like a clock hand that moves
backwards, yet can turn out as quick
as a bank transaction.
One morning when dark stays for too long,
I decide to bargain for more. Humming each lyric
aloud before trading it
off, my tongue caresses every word
that feels like stone until
it becomes the flesh of a living beast
that has tasted hard liquor for the first time, finally
aroused, ready to strike
and hunt for more —

3. Transgression

And he says,

> *Enter my body*
> *where darkness is a long,*
> *ebony lash*
> *that stops to write a sonnet at a shore.*
> *Where the land is, the sea begins.*
> *Cave into its force*
> *like the relief of a jar*
> *expanding to hold seasoned*
> *scents.*
> *Feel the flesh inside this*
> *shell,*
> *revise your space, walled*
> *with the skin of the aging moon.*
> *Not a word.*
> *Just a sudden kick of the decimal*
> *clock,*
> *syncopating*
> *the runs of your heart.*
> *Wild like a gazelle,*
> *it turns in circles.*
> *Calm it down at undivine*
> *measures, in nonlyrical*
> *conditions.*
> *All you need is to augur the distance.*
> *One road, one hand, one theater.*
> *Lure the dragon*
> *out, it is sober. Fire*
> *from its tongue*
> *will lead you back in —*

now, wake up and call
it sleep,
you've crawled,
you've fled — you've thrown yourself
into a tragic butterfly.

4. Limbic Coda

Fly. Wounded wings. A vulture wants to kill. Up the clouds.
Looking for the sun. Starts to bleed. Struggling upward. Don't
give up. Body spins. Forward thrust. Smoke engulfs eyes. Bartok's
symphony. Lower, but I fly. There are continents. Skyscrapers.
The world stretches. I grow legs. Lightning rods. Temperatures
plunge. Raining books and potatoes. Windows. Mid-air. Now I'm
on the floor. Cat meows. Husband mumbles. Sleeping on his
stomach. Forgot the alarm. Jotting down my dream. Every detail.
Head hurt. Must persevere. For example. He was cooking curry
fish before I lost the sky.

Clair de lune

The prelude banished moonlight.
                Z. tore each chord with shadow hands.

Every slipped note spoke
              like tongues for his muted thoughts.

He bulldozed silence between each quavernote
              with hiccups and strange gestures.

Let me use plain words: what you're reading
                  isn't romantic.

A tired vagabond, song clenched between his teeth.
           Moonlight filtered through like fingerbones.

Pearl

Mother begged me to bring you
home. Her face, a pale dirty
moon as I mentioned the peace
you've found in a temple where silence
woke the pine that stretched over the night.
We sat in the salon. Pots of bald bonsai
fingered into emptiness. Slices of her last
sentence crumbled in the air. Her cluttered
mind flew on wings and murdered
my words. Her gaze became yours,
it slashed through my spine. It wasn't
sudden. It was difficult. She insisted
that you practiced denial. My tongue
gagged, I dipped into cold tea
a lemon tart. A lump of sugar sank
to the bottom of my cup. It was your
body. It was my heart.

Come Back

Our waning moon paces
behind the silver
      body of the airplane.

Wind scissors the air.

White mask of death,
         a peeling hieroglyph

        Wrong night
to travel, insists my fever.

       Served cold noodles,
I press my pencil
       against the brown

       postcard. My sentence —
there is no sentence.
        Light flickers, it tries

to whisper. Sleep takes care
          of my inner animal.
I can't bury clean

bones of night. You're gone

       like a memory detail

a stretch of water, a tide that breaks but just can't turn.

III | *Not Thinking About the Past*

After the Moon

Scooping up handfuls of fresh
silence from a mirror of oblivion,
I gather from the well
that night disguises his guests.
It pleases him that wind
must wait. Even rain. Misled,
the tempered dark takes a false
step. So many shadows,
so few ghosts — I am lonely
but curious
in this imperfect end.

Refusing Lyricism

This sadness in me isn't mine. An earthern jar, Emily Dickinson, a bed.

This wait, most of all — the space, a cell that ran on dark feet in my mind. If the wait is sinister, change yourself to hours. Time is something fickle, do you deny. Taking each second personally, I chanted in Sanskrit and drew a minotaur on each wall. So badly, so well. My American friends write poems on war — political and spiritual. Is their imprisonment a subject, a word, or an example. I've lived through both, childless and don't need lies.

Jeux d'eau

Until the quavers become feathers of a fountain, Ravel remains a
beast that charges through the room. G sharps and B flats are
four times as restless. Phrases unshapely, notes flutter like fish
out of an aquarium. Arpeggios, says Martha, must be water,
touched at room temperature and without edges. Staccatos are
black stones you go inside. You can't jump too high, you must
weigh less than the stones. I am nine and here is where wisdom
should begin. *Très doux. Très expressif. Très rapide.* I am working on
three ways to enter a fountain. I found five. Imagine butterflies
in a lightful dome. Imagine clouds a belt around your waist.
These are the best two to sustain the flight. To spend the pedal.
To betray the title. If only I knew fountains never look the same.

Visitor

After the returned mail, the ruined meals, no one expects my
enthusiasm. In the streets, people hang apostrophes on their faces.
Most respond politely, but in commas. Past the stage of being
understood, or having understood, I am in a novel my father
narrated. *What's your name? Where're you from?* The heart beats a
little slower when you think you are nearer an answer. Even
windows are made of noodles and buns. Make a right turn when
a course is run. Wandering in cloisters that breathe with trap
doors, I am moving in a subjective time. Tea egg vendors fan their
stoves, they count their coins in long gowns of smoke. The poor
practice contentment because they must. How the past not mine
comes back faster than old fears. In the French Concession my
grandmother met her first love and bought a dog. After marrying
a Communist she learned to be sparing with passion and images.
How old were you, Nainai? Hungry, she answered. I thought I should
keep the afternoons free. The mornings, alone. The first night I
arrived in Shanghai, I dreamt of walking down a white
boulevard free of little madmen who looked just like me.

My 1980

John Lennon died.
I started to visit museums.

From Aesop's fables, I learned to *hold a wolf
by the ears.*

My first Latin expression: *cod ad cor loquitur.*

Later it became *acta non verba.*

Moustache, I thought, can be poetic license.
On whose face does it matter?

I collected pens with tails of sacred plumage. They
wrote on leather with an inability
to express their silence.

An interest in toilet bowls. And who sat on where.

Alone, I took elevators
holding toy soldiers. A milkman walked in,
a dairy carton on his head. He spotted my new shoes,
I saw his fingernails.

Freed from prison, Mother came to visit us
in London.
Waiting at the school gate with chrysanthemums.

Aunt Marguerite enrolled me in acting classes.
I learned to switch on tears in sonnets
of Shakespeare,

avoiding drama every now and then.

Before the Museum of Waiting

There hangs the window where I spent my twenties,

slicing oranges,
living between cigarettes and unfinished

fiction. I learned Vivaldi's concertos
by heart and stopped writing

letters to my Jewish godmother. Sometimes,
the city woke up

before kiosks opened.
My newspaper never arrived on time.

Walking past this brownstone, you ask if I miss
this life in parentheses,

shortchanging sincerity with plans
and auditions. I dip my finger

into your gelato, and pretend to think
hard. Wondering if our tall

rosewood highboy still wobbles
behind the curtains, I guess there needs

no answer for the past.

Lights turn green, you're in front.
I'm pulled back by absent-

mindedness, visualizing those whitewashed
walls, their boneless maps

and snakes' eyes, where I scribbled
lines, over and over,

between hiccups
and stammering cracks of light —

Nights are long and insomniac.
Night can also be magisterial.

Not Thinking About the Past

1. 117 W. 75th Street

Take a closer look: the rain-streaked windows
sentenced us to this verse.
                              I know — this town

holds no sentiment. The phone rings deep
in the apartment. No one here speaks French
in the right tenses. No

one sins

unless advised.

2. St. Albert's Trail

The heavy sun is down
like the day before.

A humming silence
in its departure.

Stars and the last migratory
birds — neither misty nor flexible.

I live slowly here.
Waiting for mail, thinking with pleasure.

Each day, a lesson
about erasure. You can feel

with nothing. Fiona, which
fox returns in secret?

In Edmonton, snow can't invent
snow. It has many

names, falling and rising
at neutral angles.

3. Block 33, Jalan Bahagia

two photographs

walls wrapped in vermilion, free of calendars

long windows, haute couture of an urban kampung

Peranakan tea, a kerosene lantern

like two instants from a silent film

but voices stay tender in my head

a quilt tucked in, sleeping by a cello

in this picture

riding my carousel in the other

4. 16, rue Séguier

Even stairways appear suicidally
lovely.
We resume the lives of the bourgeoisie.
Keeping the virtues, and
our distance.
The smell of herbs from the kitchen
I walk across
eight or nine times in the day.
Once,
I invited a homeless man
who insulted me in a ceremonial way.
I made tuna sandwiches
and didn't disagree.
He mended my door on a broken
ladder. *Wind,*
he said, *can now enter.*
In this large city, I am not large
but I own
a second body.
My first time —
a wheel of breath intact in my
restlessness. And
you carry me, without nostalgia.

Digesting an Academic Symposium, Some Months Back

Irony begins with the topic chosen —

Freedom, Fate and Prognostication.

Only a handful spoke in plain words.

I was grateful
because I was invited.

Took two aspirins at each breakfast.

Someone came with her pet maltipoo, paraded
naked with semi-confidence.

Her eyes, the saddest among all
participants. I looked straight into them, a madness
that could derange plants
and lovers.

Everyone ordered the Nuremberg sausages.
A cultural must-eat.

My husband revolted after the German wine.
Mein Deutsch ist nicht sehr gut!

The moon one night — unbearably white.

I even shook the hand of a scholar who spread
rumors about my lives
in Malaysia.

To conceal jealousy, he wore dark glasses, took
pictures with a pen camera. To be posted
on a blog, in a third-person account.

Is Foucault in season?

The most interesting lectures, from those who
chose to stay the peripheral sort.

For instance, an American who studied nature.

Or the Irish dramaturge in awe of Brecht
and Buddhist grottoes.

A professor emerita
trying to seduce with her foxy hairstyle

a clique of *amis*
who could handle theoretical smiles.

After the party, nothing happened.

I wasn't one of them. I wasn't difficult.
No one
harmed me, and I didn't suffer.

Trouville, 2011

By the sea the past comes tiding from toes to fingers. Rising or
falling, we hear the break of us. We come to heal because a child
left us. Can't you see the horizon in many lines. The sun arrives
on time and leaves on the mark. Let's pray for a harbor that has
no owner. With sand and oyster shells I stage an opera. In castles
and mansions devoid of persona. I stick half-cigarettes in the wet
sand. Play soldiers who prey on fear and slowness. They're trying
to breathe, but the struggle is permanent. I'll control the pain,
make the scream formless. With confused trees and gods, the
world is a budget theater. For a long time we have not been alone.
Room after room, people walk in and out. Most of them need
something from us. Perhaps I'll eat mussels marinières tonight.
With or without fries. It is too early to predict movement.
Do you really know how to feel empty. Nine times out of ten,
it is an accident. One sand castle falls, then more. And all.

Return to Self

not in order of importance

The whiteness of this page can't appease my hurt.

In the *Letter to His Father,* Kafka wrote about Hermann's threat, *I'll tear you apart like a fish.* Writers copied it in their diaries.

My sister accepts her ordainment with joy. She learns that we are traditions, we will die. I believe in myths and write love letters with leaves.

Last night is always more poetic than last year.

A colleague plants sadness in her head. To continue her dark novels, to cry with her mouth gagged.

My government is eager to give me two passports.

The smell of truth from Asia Minor — sachets of herbs and pumpkin seeds, sun-dried after the hunger strike.

Queens question velvet and monarchs.

What can you offer the sun this morning? Only the sun performs what it must.

My paper wraps my fire — this isn't a title. An observation two summers back, immortalized in an elegant measure. Of smallest clarity and skeptical music.

On Mondays, Susan phones, *Questions must need question marks.* In event of doubt, what should I do

To centralize or to italicize. There is no color.

Some of my friends write from a prison in their minds. I am happy and complete sentences. They ask me why.

The bigger your mole looks in the mirror, the more your body parts with lofty ideas. This is why Granny claims moles are temples. When I practice calligraphy, each splotch reminds me of a deformed atom.

With a diploma in healing orchids, I invent the way of healing her.

To quote a French humorist, *God is absent, but the concierge will return.*

We like the dirty goats approaching our bus-stop. Our bus is late, so are they.

Inspired by hibiscus Li Shangyin wrote, *Were there no sister inside the moon, / surrounded by clouds, a master // Three pure spheres and immortal islands / What is the reason for your exile?*

In a blue dream, I was a reptile with nine tails. If you blinked nine times, one of them would spark off an erotic house dance.

These days I speak English to a French mirror. When I exhale, the consonants shrink into an outlaw I bedded when the moon was old.

I gave my dog some avant-garde food.

At this table we dine like the nobles, exiled or not.

Mark shares the same birthday as my husband. Both live with poems and modern women. They polish silence, do not measure words, and are madly in love with camels.

In my poems, conjunctions are quiet. Prepositions serve their sentence.

I know how to live with my ambitions. It has to do with kindness and this confession.

In our bodies breed a place for spiders — we fear them, they can't forgive us.

This is a low-key departure. Observe the rites, but don't mourn. By tints and degrees, consider this death a ghost poem.

After my wake, Philippe will give away my twenty-eight hats and five jars of wrong buttons. At twenty-six, he freed lives from radios. At sixty-two, he sought pigeons and spoons.

My heart plays volcanic stone.

In the table of contents, you are still alive.

At 1 a.m. I vote for a faith. This is my secret. And my fox.

Our house, guarded by a sabre. Honor this, them, *us,* and alas.

Acknowledgments

Several of these poems—sometimes in slightly different versions—first found a home in *American Literary Review, Antigonish Review, Bitter Oleander, Compass Rose, Eleven Eleven, Ellipsis, Mānoa: A Pacific Journal of International Writing, Paris/Atlantic, Stand Magazine,* and *Tiger's Eye.*

The epigraph is translated by Randy Blasing and Mutlu Konuk. The lines of Li Shangyin in "Return to Self" are translated by Chloe Garcia-Roberts.

I must thank Susan Thomas, Jeffrey Greene, Barbara Yien, Sally Molini, Lee Sharkey, Mark Strand, and Frank Stewart.

To Ph. L.— for the hand that bows before a glove.